The House of Clay

PETER MCDONALD was born and grew up in Belfast. As a student, he won the Newdigate Prize and an Eric Gregory award. He has taught at the universities of Cambridge (where he was a Fellow of Pembroke College) and Bristol (where he was Reader in English Literature), and has been Christopher Tower Student and Tutor in Poetry in English at Christ Church, Oxford, since 1999. A prominent critic of modern and contemporary poetry, he is the author of many articles and reviews: his prose books include critical studies of Louis MacNeice, of modern Northern Irish Poetry, and *Serious Poetry: Form and Authority from Yeats to Hill* (OUP, 2002). He directs Tower Poetry, an educational initiative for the promotion of poetry and criticism, and is editor of its monthly web publication, *Poetry Matters*. He has edited Louis MacNeice's *Selected Plays* (OUP, 1993), and a new edition of MacNeice's *Collected Poems* (Faber, 2007). He is the author of three books of poetry: *Biting the Wax, Adam's Dream* and *Pastorals*. Peter McDonald lives with his wife and two children in Oxfordshire.

Also by Peter McDonald from Carcanet

Pastorals

PETER McDONALD

The House of Clay

CARCANET

First published in Great Britain in 2007 by
Carcanet Press Limited
Alliance House
Cross Street
Manchester M2 7AQ

A CIP catalogue record for this book is available from the British Library
ISBN 978 1 85754 871 6

The publisher acknowledges financial assistance from Arts Council England

Typeset by XL Publishing Services, Tiverton
Printed and bound in England by SRP Ltd, Exeter

for my mother
Sarah Louisa McDonald

Acknowledgements

I am grateful to the editors of the following publications where some of these poems first appeared: *Metre, Oxford Magazine, PN Review, Poetry Review, Thumbscrew* and *The Times Literary Supplement*.

'Flex' was first published in the pamphlet *As If* (Oxford: Thumbscrew Press, 2002). 'Mar Sarkis' was included in Marius Kociejowski (ed.), *Syria: through writers' eyes* (London: Eland, 2006).

Contents

San Domenico

My road from the bus–stop
takes me up twenty feet of steps
between high concrete walls
infested with scrubby dust and wasps,
graffiti, litter–falls,
and everywhere, from feet– to head–height,
gouged and scored, cut left and right
with bullet–holes

from fifty years ago
worn–in and weathered, that will stay so
for another fifty years,
where lizards scoot and insects go
forth, and back and forth
from shade to sun, while no one sees,
busy all afternoon for centuries
in the hot earth,

as I walk a few yards
down a line of stunned or basking cars
and the silent hospital,
then gates, and their stone eagle–guards
that look straight down the hill
as they take the longest of all long views
on walking men, just small enough to lose,
who hug the wall

as shelter from the sun
that burns straight down without reason
in the day's dead part,
and go home for the afternoon
to wait in shuttered light
half–reading books already half–read
with fruit and water and dry bread
and no appetite –

my destination too,
where I wait it out, as I have to,
with papers and ornaments
I can look over and look through,
a pile of cards unsent,
maps, glasses, and a handful of leaves
I cut this morning from three graves,
a kind of present

to myself, part souvenir
and part *memento mori*, laid out where
they wait to age and dry;
in the few hours till I appear
again on this last day
I open and close old books of lives,
smoothing their pages, to fill the first leaves
with leaves of bay.

The hand

1

A flat right hand: four fingers and a thumb,
and poised, as though to strike an instrument,
fend off a blow, or maybe stop the waves.

Each evening, it would blatter on the glass
of our front window like a thunderclap,
not breaking it, stretching our nerves past breaking.

2

Thirty years on, and I can't not drive
in this direction, just to see the place.
There's nothing much here, nobody about:

Stormont up in the hills, unearthly white
as ever, new houses eating up the fields;
but I forget more now than I remember.

Leaving, I see the parti-coloured kerbstones
with paint from last year or the year before
that fades into this almost-constant rain,

then, on one gable-wall, a raised right hand.

3

It took a full two minutes to run down
from the bus terminus to our front door:
in the last year, I skipped and swerved and darted

all the way back, with tiny ricochets
of stones at my legs and heels. All spring
I ran, and ran so fast I couldn't stop.

4

We lived in 44A Woodview Drive,
across the road, and just a few doors down
from an apprentice murderer, who learned

his trade in town, and then came home for tea.
The hard skin in my palm is like soft stone:
as I look at it now under the desk-light,

calloused and scuffed and bitten and worn-in,
this part of me is guiltless flesh and bone,
whatever it has done or might yet do.

5

Leaving means going away for the last time,
unnoticed now, hardly worth noticing:
up in the distance, Stormont, unearthly white.

I forget more than I remember – how
this road connects to that, the way to town,
the names of people who lived there, or there.

As I move faster, everything speeds up:
I make the rain stop by raising my hand,
and sunlight loses itself on the Castlereagh hills.

As seen

The house of stone,
too visible
in its one field,
dumb as a sign
you see for miles,

without a purpose
or a purpose long
gone, not known,
is always now
no home to us

now home is gone,
like the last field
of stone and clover,
and there's no sign
of us, or for us,

in that place, where
the visible ground
rises for miles,
then without purpose
it goes down

beneath the horizon
to pitch and turn
with an invisible
cargo of bodies
that pitch and turn

and that run rings
around the sky
till dusk or dawn
(no more than in
the way of things),

so no one sees
except ourselves
the dark and plain
lights in a mesh
of wires for miles

and in desperation
we force ourselves
to our bare flesh
again, and again
in desperation

as a dumb sign,
but miles away;
the tangled cry
not ours, not known;
the house of clay.

Cetacea

1

There and then, he takes a big breath

and pelts across the wooden floor
which is also the Atlantic Ocean,
to surface in front of everyone
dumbfounded on the near shore,
hoisting water by the ton
as a weightless, fast Leviathan
who cuts through elements, and sails
along with the sea-shouldering whales.

2

Late summer air: not a breath.
Across town the invasion bells
are silent, as heat coats the hills
to make them wave and tremble; hares
and birds lie low in fields of corn
while the one sound that he hears
is his own voice with the same phrase
falling in wild woods forlorn:
a little dead march that replays
its slow, unshoulderable weight,
portending sickness in the state.
Forlorn. The very sound of that.

3

Sea creatures out of their element
must know about the air's weight
beneath which lungs are bent
and twisted into knots and cramps,
while all they can do is wait,
caught in some remote *impasse*
between breath and the body: this
carries with the sounding surf
into the snort and water-puff
of a beached, exhausted grampus
not able to breathe.

Clearout

So much to be got rid of, that will go
anyhow in the end – *that* doleful saw –
stares me in the face: an *imbroglio*
of hosepipes, wire mesh, and a rusted saw
with broken flowerpots and old tools below
in this particular shed, on this one day,
all mine to sort out or to throw away.

Relentless summer rain softens the wood
as I take shelter in a box of dust
and breakage, junk and waste and solitude.
Fears in solitude. The sleep of the unjust.

*

Today, my fortieth year begins to end,
and either I am taking up more space
or else the walls really do start to close
on me, and leave me barely room to stand
up straight under the rain-beat, the rain-purr;
more lost, more stuck; duller and drowsier.

*

I waken with my arms crossed on my chest
as if I were lying on a bed of stone,
in a vaulted room that points towards the east,
around me a dozen keepsakes and talismans
to see me through, however long the wait:
dolls with the heads of animals, one flat
and stranded figurine, the shadow-puppet,
pieces of brick and bubbles of clear glass,
old schoolbooks maybe, photographs.
                            These things
aren't mine, and this must be three years ago,
surrounded by some other man's belongings,
but not here – stopped in Italy for two
bad-tempered, haunted weeks, and sheltering
in the tiny chamber every afternoon,
stopped dead, pretending to be pressing on.

★

The rain stop-starts. Wood squeaks and clicks.
I bring out bin-bags and a list of tasks.

The gnat

So up he got, moving numb legs and arms
that didn't want to move, he was so tired.
Breath was one sigh recurring; in one sigh
the grief rose in his chest, and then it broke
like a wave, collapsing everywhere at once –
grief, that is, for the gnat
                              whose ghost had spoken
all night on the subject of death, last things,
that other world beneath the world we know
where the antique and celebrated shades,
as dead as one another, do their time
in gloomy dungeons or in strange, pale fields;
the gnat, whose well-meant bite had woken him
just as a snake, with trouble on its mind,
came sliding up from nowhere to his side;
the gnat whom, without thinking, he had swiped
into perdition with one ignorant hand –
grief for the poor gnat swelled inside, almost
to bursting, as he went about his task.

First he cleared out the brambles and the weeds
that clumped together above a trickle-down
stream of pure rainwater; he took a spade
and dug out a circle, till a round of earth
stood as a simple rampart for the tomb.
This he patched up with mosses; then he searched
out the best stones from the stony hillsides,
pink- and white-veined marble, a full dozen,
and set them up together in a ring
slowly, with minute care; next, he assembled
bulbs and slips to plant for a grave-garden –

acanthus, with roses all red and purple,
a scatter of every kind of violet
to grow among the hyacinths and rare
crocuses, below a single laurel tree;
juniper then, with marigolds, and a trail
of ivy glittering in the sun like steel;
a flowering vine, narcissi underneath,
rosemary, and the bitter herb called Patience.

Last, on a plaque, in his own silent letters,
he spelled out terms of penitence and sorrow:
the debt owed to a solitary gnat,
and this repayment, too late in the day.

from *Culex* (*Appendix Virgiliana*)

Literal

Why should it be the flesh,
its muscle stretched or plush,
and the vulnerable skin
alert or dead to touch,
holding the body in
where blood and bones attach

that rises, if it does,
unwanted or desired,
the pulsebeat as it was
in a pitted body scarred
deep with its own likeness;
why should the flesh come back

to sense, and the senses' weight
return, and the skin's lightness,
unless this body's rack
of bones and intricate
fine sinews, so degloved,
marked out the literal

truth, even in disrepair;
its sadness or tired fall
as strength and force remove;
the five senses eternal,
busy again with love's
design or love's despair?

War diary

The light of the new moon and every star
concentrates now in a reflection
of trailing grasses and cow-parsley
from a puddle; clear glass is a mirror
as the night goes up into action
on wet roads, never to return:
the country roads long since taken,
known mile by mile, yard by yard,
and still abandoned. What did I see there?
Who, maybe? Some such question.

The moth

Half-daylight, and the summer stars
come out from far back in the sky
in ones and twos, still hard to see
while a temperate, short night prepares
itself to fall, but gradually,
across and into everything
light edges now, or shines along.

From somewhere in the lilac bush,
a moth has come before its time:
it blunders between purple bloom
and shadow, with the palest brush
of its wings, grainy white and dim,
then vanishes, or moves away
from where our glances barely stay.

I imagined that I saw the wings,
throughother, tattered, broken past
mending, between shadows cast
here and there, or the scattering
japs of light where branches pressed
into each other along the shade
that flowers and our own bodies made.

Too early, and hard to notice then,
pale things get lost against the light.
The garden and its trees soon let
their shadows fatten, like those thin
designs that didn't come out right,
but waited for their time to grow –
surviving now, for all we know.

The other world

after Pindar

Wild grasses, bleached, miles of them;
no sun in the glaring sky:

it is night time, so this must be
somewhere beneath the earth.

In all-over light, for ever, the grass makes
stars and rivers and waves of the sea.

Strongman

1

Bowed down, bowed under,
in his two hands, what?
A book? Or some creature
he wants to escape
more than he wants to keep?

With eyes and palms unshut,
knees bending where the steep
path started to scrape them,
he looks in wonder
at the weightless place

2

at the weightless place
between his hands
where wings maybe clapped
this minute
and the air went out of place
while it just leapt

away, while it took flight,
whatever it was,
to fast clouds and headlands
far up from where he looks
at his hands, at a pivot,
at an empty space

3

so light air fails
and no release
comes for the eyes;
no turning away
from these things
glazed and dead

that move, that ease
themselves to heads and
limbs of men
with their skins that turn
now to feathers, scales,
and the faces of beasts.

Spoils

Our taxi sails on an open road
where they have paved the wilderness –
unending hilly scrub-land

that later I look out across,
as night falls, from the balcony
of a house in a new town,

spotting arc-lights between the sky
and the next hill, watched in my turn,
while masts of concrete and steel

frame building-sites against the moon,
darken themselves, and then grow tall,
taking their certain bearings from

a fenced road to Jerusalem:
late, and better late than soon.

The overcoat

We stop, and doors come open then
to let the early dark blow in
from whatever rain-raked platform
is just outside the lighted train,
as men who lined up in a storm
crush in to seats, bringing a chilled
February air along with them,
agents for winter afternoons
and *entrepreneurs* of the cold.

On business now, and going home,
I'm no more than a few steps from
Belfast in 1972:
the cigarette smell is the same
in the same draught, that pushes through
with men who walk in envelopes
of smoke and cold from a slow queue
and onto buses with no room
in the stops and starts, the hold-ups.

Behind me by a couple of hours,
in winter downpours, sleet-showers,
he comes by bus from Inglis's,
and the breadmen and the bakers,
to town, and waits again, and catches
the number 24 or 32
home, back over his own traces,
to a breezeblock, ground-floor
Braniel flat; to damp and mildew.

Where he hangs up his overcoat
the cold begins to radiate,
shaped out, like the body's ghost,
by the hall door at night;
and now the cold that presses past
me here is maybe a ghost's trail,
the time it fills already lost
and its place lost in an infinite
line of shapes: indistinct, frail.

On Friday nights, the coat sealed up
some toy bought from a closing shop
for a shilling or for one and six,
coming to me still cold, its shape
and size all cold, a cardboard box
with a soldier or a car inside,
and the toy and winter night would mix
together, as outside would slip
inside: with gifts, and little said.

He was late one night, and came in
quietly; quietly sat down
and ate his tea, then told us how
at work for half the afternoon
the bakery had hosted two
men with guns, their faces masked,
who lined them all up in one row
on the cold floor, to wait, locked in,
for pointed questions to be asked.

The two men left eventually.
Whoever they had come to see
that day they missed, and would find
easily on some other day;
so, standing where they had been lined
up, as if in some anteroom,
everyone talked as they stayed behind,
smoking, and wondering, and free.
Little to do then but go home.

Beside me, a grey overcoat
in the train here is sending out
a smoky aura of sheer cold
invisibly in the carriage-light;
but when I get up, and take hold
of a case packed with dead papers
and a book or two, I come home late,
weighed down with chilly racing cars
and with brittle plastic soldiers.

A schoolboy

The struggle of the fly
in marmalade might have been
less hopelessly in vain

than the hopeless struggle
to right itself and fly
of my captive bluebottle

held down by the blade
of a modelling knife:
all the signs of life

were showing, to no end,
while I pressed it for blood
with a heavy hand,

and it leaked eggs and ichor
in the romper-room,
the torture-floor

where I was at home –
the legs, the tiny head
working, working away

to the very last,
when it was beheaded
by the wicked schoolboy

in whose direction I cast
this baleful stare,
a theatrical glower,

as if that could pretend
a love of the world,
of true things, not fiction,

the given, not the willed;
as if to order guilt, and
serve it in action.

Windows

1

The square shop-window (not really
a shop – a single retail-unit
let by the quarter) has been given
a once-over with a wet cloth
and thin whitewash, so that circles
loop on each other and overlap
in pale and dirty greys, the swirls
making no pattern: somebody
wrote backwards with his finger from
the inside, in not quite English,
LAST DAYS ALL MUST GO,
before he closed the door on it all
and took away what hadn't gone
some night when the last shop had shut.

2

The window-lights in Queen's Arcade
were starting to go out, as I
pressed my nose and fingers hard
up against the cold plate glass
of a sweetshop, where biscuit bears
in cartoon icing seemed to prance
and wave at me from the inside;
for minutes then I screamed and wept
to have those bears from the closed shop,
while the glass bloomed with breath and tears
around my handprints, and outside
the streets were starting to light up
on a Saturday night, drizzle-glazed
for headlamps where they came and went.

Three rivers

for Louisa

Isis

When you were born, the night sky broke to let fall
its rainwater for hours, and then for days,
then for a week at last, a week of rain,
so that I drove you home over a causeway
with fields submerged on either side of us
where the river spilled across and kept spilling,
the same river that twenty years before
I walked beside on a late October morning,
homesick, crash-landed, watching the slick water
and hearing over and over the words, *How like,*
How like, How like an angel came I down,
straining my eyes in case they broke with tears;
the river that seemed once to swell in sunlight
when it ran like an illuminated margin
beside me later, and the step-by-step
inevitable love, which started here
and brought us here, held safe and moving fast
on a road over acres of floodwater,
sending us home through rain and daylight fall.

Lagan

Down, step by step, and along the bumpy path
he used to follow here, day in, day out,
I took by the arm at last, slow and unsteady
in the blank sunlight of the seventieth spring
since he had lived here in a river cottage
now gone for ever, like that spring itself,
your grandfather, who leaned on me, and looked
through me towards the place at another time –
his run and walk and run all the way to town
along the river, or the soldiers training
across that field, who had to run until
their feet bled; or some other time entirely,
when it is you who take me by the arm
to bring me slowly past Shaw's Bridge, and past
Minnowburn, to the spot where the cottage was,
an old man who moves gently and with pain
talking to you in silences and sounds:
as afternoon lets in the sound of the river,
you help him down the worn and bumpy towpath.

Jordan

We saw the big grey fish deep in the river
as shadows and reflections from above
where we sat on the bankside steps at last,
letting the water slip into our hands
and watching colours come to near the surface
of creatures so small they were hardly fish
but green and gold half-lights, dissolved there
glittering at angles in the straight-down sun
– *How bright, How bright* – that searched the shallow bed
until the sky was shining underneath us;
the quickened surface and deep calm below
were imaged in each other, we in them,
two bodies made of frail and heavy earth,
one bending up to scoop the busy water
into a bottle held firm in the light –
your mother, who moves with you, step by step,
across the sky from one bank to the other
on a well-worn, inevitable path
that goes waist-high and waist-deep in the river.

The pattern

1

A door too low to be a door:
on the threshold
        a stepped slab
he stands first where I'm standing
not first not last
        and then inside –

or so he must have stood.

2

One step another step
                or every other
repeats itself along the dark,
the slip and pock and blip
of a line on black
screens, arched over like
a tunnel
        this tunnel
where every step
        the first the last
is every other step.

3

Crusader vaults, basalt-black,
and a flight of stairs carved down,
a sweep
        cut block by block
takes me beneath the ground
        takes him with me
already here, far under
the twisting olive trees
that clutch thin soil and dust
behind, above us both
barrelled together in the rock.

4

This is the very door
— no door, a gate
with light far behind —
and the very place
        the place here
to stand and wait
in the dark and heat
        together here.

5

He scarcely watches me
          a child
who stares into the fire
where coals burn down
to crumbly ash in the grate,
and drop into heaps of ash.

6

No door ajar
       and no one here
but me, my every step
already to be taken
       taken already,
knee-deep
in ashes that fall from bars
       above my head,
— fall like snow-smuts
from the bars of the grate
neither cold nor hot —
       my head laid bare.

Syrian

Beside a road that belts through the desert,
are a scatter of children, three or four dogs,
and, further back, a few goats, or sheep,
with the women out of sight
inside those far-off, conical houses
made out of clay, the shape of beehives:
and that's more or less everything.

The thousand-km turning to Baghdad
has been and gone, but now, all day,
a straight road goes straight on to Palmyra:
vacant remains chiselled into the sunset
and the oasis-line of palms, a palm-tree
wall blocking out Tadmor, and that
prison nobody knows or talks about.

I will rise with the sun, and walk
for half an hour across cleared ground
into ruins cluttered at the desert's edge,
hiding there among cold
stones as they start to heat up for the day
(not hidden, though, and in that
respect at least unlike too many)

while clay houses and stone houses collude
with silence and bare daylight: that combination.

The fob-watch

If I searched, my search for it was brief:
a minute or two in cupboard-boxes,
quick, like a vandal or a thief,
and there it was, the silver still
untarnished, and its rounded, milled
winder over an axle, or an axis
on which this circle turned and turned,
decades ago, in my own hand.

I must have brought the watch with me
en route for Dundonald hospital,
wanting its shape, solidity,
and heaviness all close to hand –
a face I could just understand
for what it was, learning to tell
the time, and watching little else:
the seconds, and their even pulse;

the minute-hand with its thin point
which, staring hard, I could see move
across the dial; and the faint
hint, the faint hope, proffered in one
short arm, that might be moving on
as I was looking, hard to prove,
while I searched the ivory face, to show
the time left, or time still to go.

Transfixed in bed, I hardly spoke
to visitors, or glanced at them;
I was the boy whose patient look
rested beyond all apprehension
on the fob-watch with a pure devotion
to cased and ornamented time
diminishing before my eyes:
a known and true and solid size,

weighed up again now in my palm,
as the closed shape is closing in
on all the tiny, packed and calm
world of a stopped mechanism,
where the dark backward and abysm
recede untouchably, all gone
from substance, weight; from everything:
time is time left, diminishing.

Against the fear of death

As the car boils
with sunshine, stuck,

and my hand feels
around the slippery

pudge and stubble
of my own chin,

in the heat again
that sweetsour smell,

your forehead chill
to the touch with sweat,

our two heads then,
our two faces

(ages past, the same
as now, or just then),

mine against
your frightened face

like the white pages
at the end of a book,

between gasps of pain
as we just waited,

and out there, behind
the slatted blind

that put light in threads
across your eyes,

a bright-blotted sky
too white to look at.

Mar Sarkis

I sampled the priest's home-brew
and his tapes of the Lord's Prayer
recited in strong Aramaic
(the original, for all I knew)
before trying out the stairs
cut in rock, and the tiny door

so low that I had to stoop
into candle- and mosaic-
light, then stop
for twenty minutes, half an hour,
in front of Bacchus and Sergius;
there on the stone floor,

watched by those two imperious
big-eyed, mounted soldiers
whose haloes had worn through,
I said words like a foreigner:
I bent double in grief
and prayed for your life.

In heaven

The distance starts to glow,
half-solid now,

and shapes step slowly
out, one by one,

from the horizon,
then they soften

into drumlins, row
upon neat row

of saplings, head–
high, barely moving,

and we walk side by side,
as if our hands touched,

through the small fields;
through the small fields

side by side.

★

Neither farm- nor townland
nor unapproved road;

neither fields of the dead
nor the holy ground

once more, for the light
is not the same:

the horizon round
blushes, and even the air

is larger, so we wear
clothes made of the light,

and the sun
we see by is our own;

and the many stars
when they start to shine.

Inventory

White walls and ceilings; a pallor of wood;
light from no quarter, as broad as it's wide;

daylight – not daylight, but everything else;
two shapes on the bed, one true and one false;

the quiet of clock-time repeating itself
on steel-clear mirrors on no one's behalf

but for everyone's good, while the work goes on
with nobody here, or you here alone

to take down the names from a brilliant wall,
to polish and burnish, and not bewail

the uncountable dead, with their elegies spun
thinly to nothing, and bleached to oblivion,

though not on your time. Categories shift
where the strips of beech-wood are whited and stiff,

and light at no angle gives no quarter
to glasses or blinds or shadows on plaster

as letters come round in backwards reflection,
jumbled, untouchable, sometimes uncertain,

with particulars glaring: the fall of a sparrow;
the bringing together of technique and sorrow.

The anniversary

A whole year since.
My first-thing glance
of winter today:
our stretch of grass
gone pewter-grey,
with the trees exposed
and brittle with cold;
one silent road
white as a graze.

Close up, my breath
thickens the glass;
it blooms and smears,
then fades as fast
as it came: and there
are the slippery path,
some yards of bare
hard soil, and the cars
blinded with frost.

Forecast

How everything cools and calms, how it all
tones down; how recall and forgetting
feel much the same: how the full
moon tints itself orange for a storm
as strength builds through my own right arm
pointlessly, now its fighting days are gone,
put back like everything else, and forgotten.
I hold on to you with both arms
as the rain scatters and settles in:
how everything cools and calms;
how it all tones down.

Flex

It is not the man within:
what you see when you see
the muscles through my skin
is more and less than me,

so touchy to assay
its temper and my mood,
and itching now to flay
itself, a thing of blood,

the muscle-man will walk
out of his envelope
to bad dreams with no talk
as a bunched and turning rope

that strangles, if it wants,
and squeezes to the bone
the brittle thing it haunts,
and the soft stuff within,

the will to stretch or push
feeding itself through miles
of sinew, and the lush
fibre of pumping cells,

that can neither see nor care,
can only move,
cannot cry in despair
or joy, or cry for love,

but go to their one end
without pause or dissent,
past lover and past friend,
to each indifferent.

The walk

Boundless east wind
from an empty plain;
sleet rakes the water
over itself, and back in;
the sky is a theatre
of storm- and sunlight,
long jagged cuts
of diamond in slate,

and nobody has stood
long upright, under
that sky, who did not go
down with heavy
steps on heavy steps,
with pain
like a bundle of stones,
into the fast river,

and walk, as walk he must,
breathing the dense and rainy
flat slaps of the air,
out to the very centre
of a rising flood
where it clings and cuts
with cold: it has been
a terror to many.

Quis separabit

A drive along Belfast's eastern strip
on the home leg of an airport run
at lunchtime, and in blinding rain:
the windscreen's simple weep and wipe,

the roads, the houses, the estates,
all blurred and darkened, out of shape.
The rain, the steady wipe and weep,
brings half in focus, then distorts

Dundonald, and high Castlereagh,
traffic in its long runs below,
with Stormont always just in view
– a smudge of white, of white and grey –

and then the Braniel's show of flags:
as I speed past, I leave behind
an Ulster flag, Ulster's red hand
drenched up there as it slaps and flaps,

beside it – clear as day – the Star
of David, staunch beneath black skies,
flown in defiance where it flies
glaring into the backward mirror,

surviving as one mote of white
lodged like a flaw behind the eyes –
white edged with blue. The message is
a downright question: who will part

blood from blood, and who desert us,
daring to stand here, while we stand?
The road loops back, and has no end.
Here we remain, and who shall part us?

Late morning

No sign of me.
                    The thaw
as yet hardly begun,

and sunlight leaking through
a picture of the sun
in puddles blocked with ice;

the melt-water collecting
gradually; snow-crust
broken apart with grass:

I might have been a ghost,
a shadow, and not the guest
they had been expecting.

The pieces

Tail-feathers on the kitchen floor;
up on the rooflight, against the glass,
breast down
           caught as it floats away.

*

Less than an inch
from the window-flowers
bees all morning
fiddle and bump.

*

The swatted fly had come
to tell us something; now,
instead, it sees the other world
maybe it saved us from.

*

Soft resin, or gum.
Pale amber-coloured tubs
of beeswax in the sun,
unmelting by a miracle
one by one.

*

The heavy traffic
        slow enough
to see drivers' faces,
        all of them

– we were really here,
we looked like this –

        far from here
        far from this

Music inside the car
        is years away.

                    ★

Behind the glass
        and in front of the glass
there are other worlds;

sprays of blossom
        open themselves

and glare out through the glass.

                    ★

The flowers are far off and vivid
in blasts of sun, sheeted
reflections
        all the colours
of gold and bronze.

                    ★

Hot as a bread-oven
all summer every year
the building stood firm
in its squared form
of beeswax and feathers.

                    ★

The otherworldly gnat:
                    pressed down
to its last breath.

                    ★

Walls made of bronze, imagine,
not buckling under their own weight
but kept upright
by pillars, themselves made of bronze.

★

Fluff-feathers drift up to the ceiling.

★

Slow in arriving, here it is
at last,
and the freesias know,
and the window-glass, with its
warps and smears, that sees everything,
knows all about this:
                    here it is,
much as predicted, at last.

★

They were golden, but not statues,
and they sang, but not with voices
as we knew or had imagined them:
in some lights
birds with long necks,
perched over the bronze walls,
in others, a burn and blur
of gold on the bronze,

and when they sang, it was the gold that sang.

★

Love strengthening in age;
the sun, mid-afternoon,
wants to hold on.
            And the fear of death:
the extinguished
gnat, fly, buzz-bug,
far from here
            knows all this.

★

Bird's feathers
    and no bird
– a vanishing act – gone
like the feathery house
stuck together with wax
that the winds lifted
       and took away.

★

To listen and listen
to that voice, those voices,
until you die
     a stranger
with your heart pinned
up where it shouldn't be:
think of that.

★

– far from lovers,
far from children –

★

It's like this: we
were really here; we looked
like this

– far from this,
far from here –

★

In every facet of his eye,
in every glimmer-glitz,
every separate flare,

the gloom and glare
and glower of that other world.

★

Not here — far from it —
but long brought low
to a mourning drone,
small gnats
          passed down
to the world beneath,
its gold and bronze
and all the songs

silently done with,
silently gone.

                    ★

Years afterwards,
                    for years,
the resolute patrol,
step by step, eyes
on the healed-over ground,
to find and carry off the pieces.

                    ★

Roses, are they,
          and bronze-coloured
freesias in the sun?

          That tiny sound:
the bees' soft head-butts
          on the windowpane.

The street called Straight

The ceiling makes itself a low arch
deep in the house, in the house of stone,
where you stoop down, then stand up alone
with the cold of walls that are wet to touch,
and in shadows spotted with candlelight.
What holds on here will not soon let go;

it takes the air and sky, it takes your sight
away, it takes everything: you are blind and slow,
and this is still two thousand years ago,
when the body is just a dead or a dying weight
led in here from the street, the street called Straight,
under dark stones into the pressure of stone.

Bowed down, you have stayed these years, the same
weight, a deep weight, felt here, and sealed;
or else a figure cut from parched light,
seen for a moment when the moment came,
some creature made out of bone and flame,
leaving the cripple and the blind man healed.

Arithmetic

To work it through, the brain is just
two clumsy hands of fingers, thumbs,
or a contraption thick with dust
that still performs the easy sums,

imagines twenty take away
eleven, and divides by three;
takes three away; has dismal play
in asking then, for *a* and *b*

which values make the answer nil?
For now the figures cut across
each other and each day, until
the slow arithmetic of loss

becomes a reflex scarcely strange,
not useful, and unused; just there,
one way the wits can rearrange
themselves for time and disrepair,

for miles clocked up and counted down;
for always having less to say,
when every answer is long known,
and numbers take themselves away.

Vigilantes

They stand guard at the invisible gates,
solid against the dark, with covered faces:
we slow, and drive towards them in first gear
on Saturday nights, coming in from town,
then tell them our business, and who we are.
Behind us, the gates close, and we drive on.

★

Hours ahead of me, you have got up early,
and slipped out to the car, just as night ends:
my bedroom curtains tint first light
as I listen to you start the engine
and drive uphill, out of the estate,
not seeing the closed gates, but being seen.

★

You are somewhere on the far side of those gates,
and now the vigilantes with no faces
are watching as I try to slip out early
through first light, where the darkness ends,
as if I were invisible;
as if my business really were my own.

Ode

Who looks out with an equal mind
to huge and meaningless horizons,
where sea makes one long ridge of surf
over the reefs that circle us
– an enormous pallor in all directions
of oblivion once, oblivion returning
to meet at a point, and meet us there –

who sees all this with an equal mind,
knowing how pointless fear is,
and the wild unimportance of the times,
possesses himself, comes into his own
where the tyrant-postures of a future state
can cut no ice, and the ravenous past
consume no tissue from his heart.
                                        Who sees

with equable, unflappable regard
his own mind open on both sides,
as if the winds would blow through, and the stars
race through it, and the sea pour through,
is equal to the verdict, long delayed,
that comes round from the past or from the future,
returned unopened, not at this address.

44A

I was trying to recall, and find words for,
the heavy sigh of our front door

pulling shut on its air-spring,
the small, mosquito-high ringing

of a timer-light out in the hall,
and the ox-blood colour of the tiles;

all from my narrow perch abroad
at the very hour you died.

★

In the optician's chair that day
beads of light were sore and dry

as I watched for a puff of air
that would reveal the blood-pressure

inside each open, waiting eye:
the thing is not to flinch, to try

to keep a steady head; I flinched;
we tried again; again I flinched.

★

A winter's day in Woodview Drive,
much like the days when you drove

home through twilight in a Ford
Prefect, and the sunset flared

between its windscreen and the rain;
or the rusty Mini, the sky-blue Austin

eleven-hundred, cars you tended
after their best days had ended.

*

The crazy paving, a foot wide,
never cemented, wobbled outside

our front window, where I found
my balance on one stone, and stood

poised, back to the roughcast wall,
like the boy-king of the Braniel,

with toes, feet, ankles and knees
shifting my own weight in the breeze.

*

It would take the light from your eyes –
I know; and it's hardly a surprise,

it's hardly news: that I should find
cold air at the gable-end

strange, or your face then, full
of the fear of death, terrible;

outside is empty, and goes away
fast as light this winter day.

*

Dead pieces in my life begin
to join up, one by one,

and now the Braniel falls below
my feet; the houses start to go,

as I keep steady in a place
made out of distances and space;

a prodigy of balance, where
the last breath is a breath of air.

The bees

1

When the last of the sunlight goes,
and shadows stretching from the shade
of trees and bushes, long hedgerows,
join up together to invade
wild grasses and the flat pasture,
turning from shadows into night,
then the bees, scattered far and near,
take notice, and start on their flight
back to those walls and roofs they know,
beehives where their small bodies rest
between the dark and dawn; they go
over the threshold, noisy, fast,
massing in hundreds at the doors,
and pour past into their close cells,
cramming chambers and corridors
while the last of the daylight fails:
sleep silences the working hive
and leaves it quiet as the grave.

2

For bees put no trust in the sky
when storms come up with an east wind,
and seldom venture far away
from their stations when downpours impend:
instead, they draw the water off
and stick close to their city walls
where any flights they take are brief;
as the wind blows and the rain falls
they steady themselves through turbulence
by taking with them little stones
(as frail boats, faced with violence
of gales and tides, take ballast on),
and hold their given course along
the clouds, balanced, and balancing.

3

A wonder, how they reproduce:
without courtship, or lovemaking,
without letting their hearts unloose
nerves and sinews like so much string,
without the agony of birth,
they gather offspring from the leaves
and softer herbs, draw with each breath
pollen and children for the hives,
providing themselves with a fresh
ruler, and tiny citizens,
to take the place of some who crash
against the earth, onto hard stones,
brought level by their single love
for flowers, and honey-vintages
(the glorious legacy they leave
behind them, in trust for the ages),
although the time that waits for them
is short enough, and not beyond
a seventh summer; yet the same
nation and race will soldier on,
deathless in spite of time's attacks,
in cells and palaces of wax.

4

All of these things have given pause
to the bees' watchers and guardians
whenever they ascribe the cause
to some influx, some influence
over and above the natural,
an exhalation from beyond
or an element more ethereal
than air itself – maybe the mind
of God, that strengthens as it runs
in earth and sky, or turns in deep
acres of churning oceans,
in herds of cattle, flocks of sheep,
the wild beasts and the harmless beasts,
in life that feels along a thread
from its first moment to the last,
finishing where it all started,
and never reaching a true end:
this keeps the bees away from death
when, at the last, they all ascend
into the skies they lived beneath,
to fly between undarkened spheres
in heaven, and the many stars.

from Virgil, *Georgics* Book IV

τοῖσι λάμπει μὲν μένος ἀελίου
τὰν ἐνθάδε νύκτα κάτω

The light of the sun
when the sun has gone
beneath the hills
shines on them all,

but with no dawn
or evening light:
unshadowed white,
one equal noon;

while, edging near
around a hearth,
darkness here
comes up from the earth.

Notes

Some poems make use of passages of Pindar and Virgil. The book's last poem is preceded by two lines of Greek from a fragment of a Threnos, or lament, by Pindar. Along with 'In heaven' and 'The other world', it includes some free translation of this fragment. Pindar's subject (according to Plutarch, *Letter of Consolation to Apollonios* 35. 120C), is the abode in Hades of the pious dead:

> For them, beneath us while the night is here,
> there blazes down the power of the sun;
> in fields crimson with roses
> they have their suburb, and their shady trees
> of frankincense [...]
> and trees weighted with golden fruit:
> some take delight in horses, some
> in exercises, some in games of draughts,
> others in the music of lyres,
> and happiness is common to them all
> in its full bloom, completely.
> Across that lovely country the scent
> spreads out, from offerings of every kind
> they mix on the gods' altars
> with fire, seen burning from far off.
> (Pindar, Threnos 7 (fr. 129), ll. 1–10)

'In heaven' adapts a passage of a few lines from Virgil's *Aeneid*, in which Aeneas and the Sibyl, having performed the necessary rites, enter the Elysian fields:

> When they had done all of this, and obeyed the goddess's order,
> at length they came to the joyful country, covered in long grass
> and beautiful, with its holy groves, the retreats of good spirits.
> The air they breathe is larger here, and it clothes with a purple
> light those meadows; they have a sun of their own, and they know
> stars in their own constellations.
> (Virgil, *Aeneid* 6, ll. 637–641)

'The pieces' makes use of material concerning the early temples of Apollo at Delphi. In the writings of Pausanias (c. AD 150), there is the following account:

69

They say that the most ancient temple of Apollo was made of laurel, the branches of which were brought from the laurel in Tempe. This temple must have had the form of a hut. The Delphians say that the second temple was made by bees from beeswax and feathers, and that it was sent to the Hyperboreans by Apollo. [...] It is no wonder that the third temple was made of bronze, seeing that Acrisius made a bedchamber of bronze for his daughter, the Lacedaemonians still possess a sanctuary of Athena of the Bronze House, and the Roman forum, a marvel for its size and style, possesses a roof of bronze. So it would not be unlikely that a temple of bronze was made for Apollo. The rest of the story I cannot believe, either that the temple was the work of Hephaestus, or the legend about the golden singers, referred to by Pindar in his verses about this bronze temple:

> Above the pediment sang
> Golden Charmers.

[...] Neither did I find the accounts agree of the way this temple disappeared. Some say that it fell into a chasm in the earth, others that it was melted by fire.

(Pausanias, *Description of Greece* 10.5.9.–12.,
trans. W.H.S. Jones and H.A. Ormerod (1918))

I have also drawn on the fragment of Pindar which Pausanias refers to here, Paean 8. The lines I have used are these:

> The walls were bronze, and bronze
> columns stood beneath them:
> up on the pediment, six golden
> singers cast their spell.
> But when the sons of Kronos
> opened the earth with thunder,
> they buried that most sacred of all works,
> amazed at the sweet singing –
> for travellers were dying
> far away from their children
> and their wives, having set their hearts
> on that song, mellifluous, addictive.
> (Pindar, Paean 8 (fr. 52i), ll. 68-79)

The last line of 'The other world' is a literal translation of a single-line fragment of Pindar (fr. 136a.)

The first line of 'War diary' is taken from Edward Thomas's diary for 1 January – 8 April 1917, where it is found on the last pages. See *The Collected Poems of Edward Thomas*, ed. R. George Thomas (Oxford: OUP, 1981), p. 194.

The Braniel housing estate, mentioned in several of the poems, is situated in east Belfast, and is pronounced to rhyme with 'Daniel'.